My Life

My Testimony

By June Haines

Copyright Page

My Life My Testimony
Author June Haines
Artist and Illustrator: June Haines

www.fordivinepurpose.com
info@fordivinepurpose.com

Published by Olmstead Publishing
1631 Rock Springs Rd
Apopka, FL 32712-2229
407-814-8770
olmsteadllc@usa.com

ISBN: 978-1-934194-19-5

September 2007

Dedication

I dedicate this book to Apostle Matthew James Shaw and Pastor Pamela Shaw.

God has placed a mighty man and woman of God over my life. I am very blessed and honored to call them my Spiritual Parents.

They not only preach the word, they live it. My Pastors are a bible that people don't see.

I remember when I first met them at a friend's house. Whenever I would see them coming I would hide outside until they left.

I was not saved at the time, nor did I want to be. I was really shocked when I found out that my friend gave her life to the Lord.

That was not for me at the time.

My friend was battling cancer and doctors said that she was not going to be here long. Whatever she needed or wanted me to do for her, I did.

She would call me and ask me to take her to church. I would drive 35 to 40 minutes to pick her up and she only lived around the corner from the church. I see now that the Lord was setting me up

After she passed away I stopped going to the church. I was not ready to give my life to the Lord and I wasn't going to change my lifestyle.

I said God! When I am ready to serve you take me back to that place where those people are.

A few years passed and I saw them again, this time I was ready for the Lord.

My Pastors never looked down on me and they treated me like I was someone special. Whenever I needed to talk with them they would make their self available to me.

They have poured so much into my life and I will never forget it. My family is blessed to be connected to such great people.

I thank God for them because the people from Faith and Power Worship Center are a product of everything they have taught us. They won't tell us to do something that they wouldn't do themselves.

Faith and Power Worship Center

"Where the Pure and Perfect Love of God abides"

I have never had such great and humble people in my life.

Apostle Matthew J Shaw and Pastor Pamela Shaw

My Life

I was born June 18, 1971 in Lake City, South Carolina. I have two brothers that are from my mom and dad. I have a few half brothers and sisters that are just from my dad.

I was raised in Orlando, Florida where I have spent most of my life. I have also lived in Los Angeles, California and Las Vegas, Nevada.

My parents divorced when my brothers and I were very young. We were living in Canada at the time. My dad gave my mom some money, bought our plane tickets, and then sent us to Florida.

My mom didn't have any money or a job. We lived place to place with different family members. I remember when I was a little girl my mom couldn't take care of my brothers and me. She put us in a home where they took in runaways.

This was when the real pain began . . . .

The mother of the house made sure we had plenty to eat and clothes to wear. At night she would make the house girls give us a bath and, I will never forget, when the girls would line my brothers and I up. In the tub they would turn us around one at a time. They would have us touch them and they would do the same to us. They would beat us with a hanger if we didn't do what they said.

When it was time to go to sleep my brothers and I were separated. I had to sleep on the top bunk in between two girls that would wait for me to go to sleep, then kick me off of the bed onto a hardwood floor.

When my mom found out about the abuse she finally came and got us.

We moved to several different places before we got to our final stop…

It was so awesome to have a place to call home… We moved into the projects in Orlando where we were raised.

At the age of seven I remember the police coming to our door and the phone ringing we found out that my grandmother on my mom's side had passed away.

We went to South Carolina for the funeral and when we got there everyone decided that the children had to stay home with a friend of the family.

None of us minded because it was cold outside and it gave us a chance to spend some time together.

Most of my cousins and my brothers were in the living room watching TV and I went into the back room to hang out with everyone else…

I lay down on the bed for a little bit and then the man who was a friend of the family decided he was going to place his hand in my pants…

I was in complete shock and then I jumped off the bed and ran into the living room where my cousins were.

I stood beside them while they were trying to keep warm at the heater. He came over to where I was and begged me not to tell my mom or anyone. He said that if my mom found out she would kill him.

I decided not to tell my mom because I wanted to protect him and I guess I was kind of scared.

We used to watch my mom party a lot. She would come home drunk and falling down or getting sick in the bathroom.

There were many times when she left us places so she could go out and have fun.

One of those nights we had to stay at her friend's house and while she was partying I was being woken up by her friend's boyfriend's hand in my pants.

By this time I was eight years old and been sexually abused three times by three different people. There were a few more times of this with a few more people. I had become so disgusted with myself that I didn't want anyone to like me. I just wanted to be fat and ugly.

As a small child I saw too much and heard too much.

We watched our mom struggle when we were little, I know she did the best that she knew how to.

When ever she had just a little extra money she would cook us some cabbage and potatoes for Sunday dinner.

I know what it is like to go to sleep hungry and wake up in the morning and run to the fridge and hoping that someone put some food in it.

I used to look forward to the first of the month when we could get some government cheese and milk.

I had a very poor life, but I learned to survive.

I never had the chance to really get to know the other side of my family. My dad's side never really accepted us and I can count on one hand how many times we received a call for our birthdays, a gift for Christmas, or any holiday.

I wished that I had the chance to grow up with my cousins and spend time with all of my aunts and uncles. I have had the chance to spend more time with them now that I am older. Things are much better. My uncle is really good about keeping in touch.

However, I don't regret my life, or even my family, because I love each one of them.

I grew up in the projects and I learned a lot from the streets. The streets taught me how to defend myself. I became hard and bitter and to the point that I was going to get you before you got me.

I was smoking at the age of 14 years old and drinking at the age of 15. By the time I was 16 years old I was smoking weed, having sex, and expelled from school for selling drugs. I had several men that I was seeing my age and older.

I moved to Los Angeles with my dad for a while and got caught up with drugs and violence out there.

I was seeing a major drug dealer and hanging out in the clubs where gangs were getting ready to fight.

At the age of 17 I was dating another guy who was a major drug dealer who was giving me all the drugs I wanted because he was also a pimp and he was trying to turn me out (make me a prostitute).

After he was arrested and went to jail, I became pregnant with my first child. His daddy didn't want anything to do with him so he left me. I became a single mom.

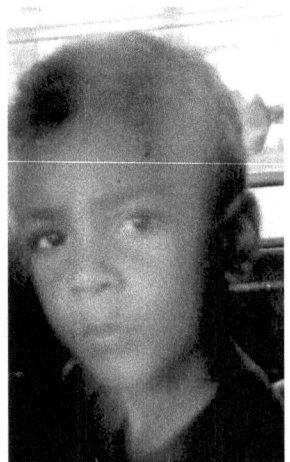

By this time I was out of control and no one could stop me.

I met this guy who I tried really hard to settle down with. I was 18 and he was 26. I figured he was mature and had a good job, why not give him a chance.

Man!!!! What was I thinking? It started out fine until I started seeing another side of him. He began to play games like "I am going to hold you down on the bed and put a pillow over your face and the only way you will live is if you take short breathes."

I figured it was a sick game but, I just didn't leave him alone. At the age of 19 I was pregnant with my second child. I had a miscarriage.

At the age of 21 I gave birth to a stillborn baby girl. I left the hospital to go straight to a funeral home to prepare a funeral for my child.

I went through so much with this man-- from having babies to constant fights.

Everyday it was something. This lasted for eleven years and five pregnancies.

Finally this had to end. I had just given birth to my youngest son. He was two months old when I left this man.

9

It was such a struggle raising these kids on my own and then I began to see the pattern of my childhood.

I was partying all the time…drinking, smoking, sleeping around, cursing out everyone and I was dating so many guys that my friends named me "Lil Pimp June." Guys didn't know how to handle me because I just did not care.

I would club all night, have sex in the parking lot or where ever I wanted.

People who knew me knew I was crazy and not afraid of anything.

After years of partying, struggling, I was at a place in my life where I was so ready to just give up.

My Testimony

God STEPPED right on in and took over from there….
I have had a chance to tell you some of what I went through in my life, now let me share with you my testimony.

I had planned a fun weekend out with my late friend's daughter. She had turned 18. I figured since I was out anyway I could take her with me.

She agreed to go out to the club, but I had to agree to go to church.

I showed up to pick her up at her God Parent's house and when I entered the door she hugged me and I was greeted by her God Parents.

We talked for a few minutes and I kept trying to watch the clock because it was ladies night and ladies drank free until midnight.

As we were getting ready to walk out the door they decided that they wanted to pray for us. WELL!!!! I let them pray and then rushed home to get ready for the club. By the time we got into the car to go out it was 11 pm….

I started the car and pushed down on the clutch and it hit the floor. I tried to get the clutch back up and there was no way I could.

After about 20 minutes of messing with this car it hit that we were just prayed for. I looked over at Christina and said "Man we let them people pray for us and now my car won't go anywhere!"

Finally, I was able to get the clutch back up and we were on our way to the club.

That night was a very expensive night because I had to pay for my drinks and pay to get in the club…

I got up early that Sunday morning trying to think of a way to get out of going to church.

After a while I just said, "Ok Lord, I have partied all weekend long I guess I can give you a couple hours of my time."

I went to church and I was watching everyone around me dancing and praising God…Then they went into worship and I was still just watching the people.

When the message came I was just sitting there and taking in every word. Apostle Matt was speaking about abundance and prosperity.

As he was talking the Spirit of the Lord spoke to me and said, "Do you want the abundance of what the world has for you or do you want the abundance of what God has for you?"

I just looked down at my hands and said "Lord, the world has given me nothing. My children have no food at home and we are struggling very hard to pay the bills." I said, "Lord! If you can do better than what I have right now then I'll give you a try, because right now I have nothing."

That day January 4, 2004 I accepted the Lord in my life. When I walked out of that service I knew my life would never be the same.

I went home and picked up my children and we went to the grocery store. I said "God I am not going to worry about these bills or anything else because I am going to buy my children some food."

I had not bought food for my home for a year and a half. People gave us food sometimes or the children ate at their dad's house before they would come home.

When we got home and started unloading the bags we saw our pantry get full, our fridge was full, and we had so much food that we had to bring the rest to my bedroom…BUT GOD!!! He showed me Ephesians 3:20 that day.

The Lord began to deliver me from things in my life little by little. The first thing he took away was a filthy mouth. I have been cursing people out since I was 14 years old.

My mouth was so bad that Jerry Springer wouldn't allow me on his show (not that I tried to go anyway).

The next thing was drinking…Praise God!!! I had all kinds of liquor in my house.

After I had my stillborn baby I would drink heavy when it was close to her birthday or holidays, because I didn't want to think or hurt anymore about losing her.

I never had a chance to heal from her death caused by medical negligence and I would sometimes get angry because I couldn't find her grave when I would finally go visit her.

The last time we went my children and I took some artificial flowers out there and spoke to someone there who took me straight to her grave and we placed the flowers there and walked away.

The Lord gave me a peace about her death and helped me to understand that she was with him and there was no need to go back to the grave.

Smoking…God delivered me from smoking. One month after I got saved….BUT GOD!!! I have been smoking since I was 14. I would quit while I was pregnant and then eventually start back up.

The Spirit of the Lord said, "Throw them in the garbage!" and I looked at the cigarettes for a minute and was trying to hold on to some just in case I wanted one later and he said it again. "Throw them in the garbage." I immediately tossed them and, PRAISE THE LORD, I have not touched them again….

I was so excited about fasting and wanting to experience the things that I heard about prayer and fasting.

I used to hear people speaking in tongues and they were filled with the Holy Spirit and I wanted that (badly).

I remember standing in the kitchen at Elder Beyrl's house and I was asking her about speaking in tongues. I asked her how I can do that. I had a tongue ring in my mouth and I said, "Do you think if I take this out of my mouth I will be able to speak in tongues?" and she said "Sure."

So, I went home and took it out and two days later I was filled by the Holy Spirit with the gift of speaking tongues.

I was so excited!!!

Now that God had delivered me from smoking, drinking, cursing he was dealing with me about being still so I could hear from him…

I had a desire for my long nails…I would not let anyone touch them. I designed my fingernails and toe nails so they matched. My toe nails were so long that I had to wear open toed shoes.

I was at home reading my Bible and I could not understand what I was reading so I said, "GOD! I know that you are trying to show me something but I do not understand." I finally got up off the couch and went into my bedroom and began watching the Christian channel.

There was a preacher ministering about the same thing that I was reading. That caught my attention quickly.
Basically what the Lord was saying is that faith is the strength that you need to cure the lusts and the desires that you have.
The Spirit of the Lord said, "Get rid of the nails!" I looked around and I said "Lord; you have delivered me from so much please let me keep the nails." He said it again "Get rid of the nails!"

I immediately cut the nails off. I called my Pastors and told them what had taken place. My Pastor said, "Sister June, you know that nails are not a sin!" I said, "I know that but because of my desire for them and how I lust for them I have made them a sin."

She said, "Ok, as long as you understand."
Well the very next day I received a call from a lady named Minister Courtney. She said, "Sister June, the Lord spoke to me and I need to come and see you." I said, "Ok."

When she arrived at my house she had a bag of paints and one canvas.

I laughed at her because I did not know how to paint and I asked, "What is this for?" She said, "The Lord told her to bring it to me."

I laughed again and said, "God must have a sense of humor, because I don't know how to paint, the art that I knew was on my

fingernails." Minister Courtney stated, "God will show you what to do with it."

Later that night I was sleeping on the couch and this picture was in my head and I could not get it out. About three hours later I said, "Ok, Lord! I will paint the picture, just please let me go to sleep."

The next morning I got up and sat at the table and picked up the canvas, I began turning it around and trying to hold the paint brush. I continued to laugh. Finally, I dipped the paint brush into the paint and began to paint on the canvas.

It was funny because as I painted it started to look like an island with water and three large clouds with a little piece of a sun shining through the clouds.

My son came home from school and I asked him to look at the picture. "I said don't laugh just tell me what you see!"

He looked at the picture and then he backed up from it and said, "Mom! I have seen this picture before in a dream when I was little."

He said, "Mom, if you bring the sand down on the painting then you will see where Moses parted the Red Sea."

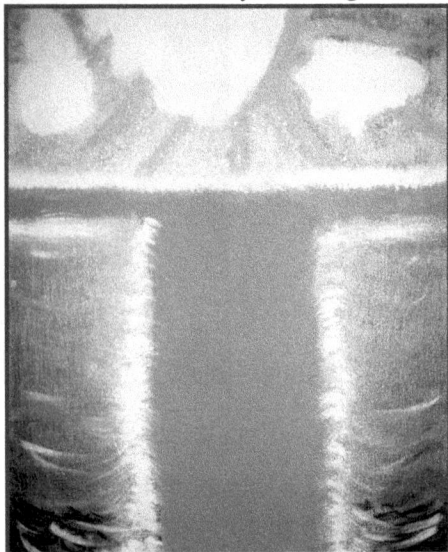

After I did that I became real excited about the picture. I called so many people and told them what just happened. How God showed me a picture in my sleep and then it was painted on a canvas. Praise God!

I called one the elder's from the Church and asked her if I

The Parting of the Red Sea
by June Haines

could bring the picture by for her to see. She said, "Sure, come on over."

While in my car driving to her house I got stuck behind a garbage truck, I stared at the painting and I looked over at the clouds then the Spirit of the Lord said, "Let your light shine so bright that people will just see you and cross over to the promise land."

From that day on the Lord has used my hands to paint. He is teaching me scriptures in the Bible, as well as speaking prophetically in the lives of other people.
I only paint when I am inspired to paint by the Holy Spirit to do so.

People call me and interpret each of the paintings. I receive testimony's all of the time about how people have seen there own personal experiences and life situations in the glass, then they see how to come out of the storm.

The Word of God said that he will give us gifts, and then bring us before great men.

I am now a Christian artist with over 200 pieces of art that are being seen all over the world. I also teach art class for elementary students, as well as college students, how to paint on glass. I have art on clothes, handbags, mouse pads, neckties, and greeting cards. God has also given me a gift to write poems. I give God ALL the glory, honor, and praise.

My Stumbling Block

I met this guy at a party and I really liked him. I said he is young and a lot of fun. I always said that the devil must have known that I was going to be saved because I fell in love with this guy and to know me there would be NO way that I would fall in love with anyone.

We had a lot of fun together and he was with me almost every night. I would be at the club until 2 or 3 in the morning and call him to say I was on my way home and he would meet me there.

This went on for a long time and then one day I messed around and got saved.

He was shocked!!

It was very hard for us because we were used to being together and as God was dealing with me about being with Carlos. I tried hard to justify my sin saying that I didn't see it in the Word of God that I couldn't be with him. I just saw the part about committing adultery. I figured we weren't married so it wasn't adultery. I went to church every Sunday and every Wednesday. I was serving God faithfully except with sleeping with Carlos. If truth be known, I was ushering in the church.

Yup, I said it…I was ushering in the church while at home I was still fornicating.

I am not bringing glory to what I did, I am saying that even though I was living as good as I could and trying to do everything right I was still living in sin.

I remember getting to church early on a Wednesday night to prepare to usher.

As I was walking around I noticed a mighty man of God just sitting there watching everyone, I walked over to him and gave him a hug like I always do.

After I hugged him he said to me with a very strong voice "Know ye not that your body is not your own, you have been bought with a price!"

I looked at him and at that moment I know the Holy Spirit was speaking through him and that God sees everything.

I walked away with such a conviction because I knew I was guilty. I went home that night and Carlos was there waiting for me. I was really going through it now because I loved God and I loved Carlos. I knew that it was coming close to the time where I was going to have to make a choice.

I held on as long as I could to Carlos. I kept praying that he would be saved and we could be together. But it wasn't happening like that.

Finally, one day at Church we had a guest speaker and I was really enjoying myself. The word was so great and the evangelist was keeping everyone excited.

At the end of the service he called my Pastors to the front and he said to them that there were people in this ministry that are close to them and that they were sabotaging this house.

After the man of God finished speaking to my Pastors I felt a pull on me like I knew that I was one of those people.

I thought I was only hurting myself if I was living in sin and no one else. Boy, was I wrong. I found out that with me being an usher and committing sin that I was contaminating the offering and sabotaging the ministry.

That hit me hard. . . . I went home and I was praying and asking him to show me where in the word it says having sex before marriage was wrong.

I would even ask questions like, "How do you just quit having sex with someone that you have been with?"

I have never been sex free so this was really hard for me. I was told to start praying for the soul ties to be broken and I did that…

I would sleep with this man because I wanted to be with him . . . and cry because I didn't want to hurt the ministry and sin against God.

I would cry out to God, begging him to take this lust and these soul ties away from me. This went on for a while and I will never forget that night…

Carlos was sleeping beside me and I was reading the word and I came across 1 Corinthians, Chapter 6. It said fornicators and adulterers will never see the Kingdom of God.

I said, "God, you mean that I can walk this walk and do everything that I know to do right and because of fornication still never make it to heaven?"

That was it for me. I said, "You got to go!! Man, I can't go to Hell for this."….He looked at me like what are you talking about! I explained to him that with us being together in a sexual way would stop me from seeing the Kingdom of God.
We tried really hard to stay away from each other but once we saw each other again it was hard to separate.

I remember one evening he asked me to stop by and I agreed because I really wanted to see him.

Carlos was so awesome through all of this because, even though he was not a Christian, he still saw God moving in my life and he didn't want to ever do anything to change that.

He said that he saw God make a 360 degree turn in my life. He has always encouraged me to go out and do what God has called me to do and I will always love him for loving me enough to let me go. I still talk to him occasionally, but it is just on a friendship level and we can both see how we have grown.

My Life Today

I have watched God move in so many situations in my life I remember when God was dealing with me about the poverty mind set that I had. I was in Section 8 housing and I knew that if I quit my job then I wouldn't have to pay rent.

I would also put myself in financial trouble and call on God to bail me out. My light bill was due and I would call on God until the last day of my extension and then, because he didn't move quick enough for me, I would go to the check cashing place and get a loan.

I was sitting in service on a Sunday and my pastor was preaching. All of a sudden, the Lord said, "If you go back to that check cashing place and take out another loan I will make it twice as hard for you to catch back up."

I heard it so clear that it almost freaked me out. The Lord said "I am doing a mind shift change in you, and it is time to BREAK that poverty mind set."

I promised God that I would totally trust him.

God began to show me being separated from my children. I kept asking God not to take them from me.

I started to get rid of things in my house that were from my past. One day at church a lady came to me and said my doors are open! I just looked at her and then I said, "Thank you."

I knew then that I would be separated from my children.

A few weeks went by and I moved in with that woman of God. My children were in two different places. This was something that was very hard to do.

God gave me such a peace about being away from my children. I would only have them on Saturdays and then I would drop them back off on Sunday. This lasted for nine months.

I never questioned God about separating my family and I trusted God enough that I knew that he would bring us back together.

I am not saying that it was easy, because I cried many of tears from missing them so much. I would pray and fast all the time for us to be back together in the same house.

I remember just crying out to God and begging him to open that door for us and it was like he didn't hear me.

One Sunday night I called a woman of God from my church who was also a real estate agent and I asked to help me find a house. My credit was so messed up and she was very honest with me. She said that she could not help me get a house but she said that she had a two-bedroom, two-bath condo and that if I wanted to move in then she would rent it to me.

Praise the Lord!!!! After nine months of being without them, God opened that door for my children to come home. We spent one year in a two-bedroom, two-bath condo and now God has blessed us with a four-bedroom, two-bath, two-story home that we are loving.

God has brought us from the pit to the palace! We have not been separated again.

I give God ALL of the glory, honor, and praise for what he has done and is still doing in my life. I have no regrets about anything because everything that I have gone through made me what I am today.

I am a MWOG, "Mighty Woman Of God," and I love the Lord with everything inside of me.

Lord, I bless your name and I thank you for My Life and My Testimony, in Jesus' name.

June Haines

I pray that everyone who reads this book is encouraged and blessed by it. Always understand that God has a master plan for our life.

There is not one thing that happens to us in life that God is not aware of.

Trust the Lord with all your heart; and lean not unto your own understanding. In all your ways acknowledge him and he will direct your paths. Proverbs 3:5-6

www.ingramcontent.com/pod-product-compliance
Lightning Source LLC
Chambersburg PA
CBHW071450040426
42445CB00012BA/1506